P9-AOK-270

EARLY RISING

Early Rising

CHARLES DAVID WRIGHT

THE UNIVERSITY OF NORTH CAROLINA PRESS
CHAPEL HILL
1968

Some of the poems in this volume originally appeared in *The Carolina Quarterly, College English, Harper's Magazine, The Kenyon Review, Lillabulero, The New American Review, No. 4, The Saturday Review,* and *The Southern Poetry Review.*

TO
O. B. HARDISON, JR.

CONTENTS

EARLY RISING

EARLY RISING

Weeks when no grass stood high enough in graveyards
nor culverts cracked to spread the Public Works
over six days, my dad made bread, shaping
the dough in the dark morning while we slept,
gone with that great basket over his arm
before we woke. But once, I saw what he sold
still slick white in gray larded pans, ready
beside the oven. Out of a bad dream
breaking safe awake, I saw light cracking
under the kitchen door and came to watch.
Sweating and floury white as mime or clown,
my funny father stood hiding his hands
in working dough. He squeezed my nose yeasty
and set me on the stool beside the stove.
Between day and night his knife divided
it all. He made loaves with his hands,
the way I made with mud, and he greased the pans.
If the loaves and the sun rose, I don't remember.
The warmth of his bright business hummed
stronger than song or rocker and it pulled
like a pillow, down and down.
                              High into noon,
I watched him from our maple coming home,
this time to stop, this time to eat the bread.
He showed some little cash and a basket full
of barter—goose eggs and sweet ears of corn,
green onions and a root of sassafras.
He made a moustache at the dinner table,
the cornsilk sticking to his sweating lip.
I laughed in my beans at my funny father.
But funniest of all when his eyes closed
and his face lowered sleeping to the plate.
I sang, "This is the way we bake our bread
so early in the morning" in his ear,
till he rose out of his sudden dream and ate.

THE BEARINGS GAME

Seven years and half
a cornstalk high, I
used to run a random
rout eyes aground all
over a quarter in corn, till
in a green snarl of snakes
and ladders I raced with time
out of mind, trying to keep
the furrows unfamiliar, to undo
the plower's plan, for wilder
and wilderness' sake. So I spelled
myself into a hazel of hunches
who could, without telling
by tips of token trees,
home out where I came in.

When all true notions worked
then home was a happening
and where I simply stood
a little unlikelyhood.

THE BALE

Up like a dust devil rose
hay prices all the drought
year, till keeping our cow
for milk saved little money.
With no pasture and the yard
cropped close and grass forgotten,
at last one bale was charged.
In some public ditch my father
was heaving mud for hay money
and Mother with her basket gone
gleaning our neighbor's dandlion greens
when the bale came. It stood
taller than me, until my dog
barked at it and I tipped it
over. Then it was a hill,
a whole field all huddled
in cunning wire for the bent
of raggling dogs and capsized kings
of the castle, hayday's shifting
trampoline. How could it hold
its sides or half contain itself?
One last wanton roll left
nothing undone and all over.
Worrying the baling wire in
his clay hands, my father
studied our scattering in the gathered
dusk, and then the taut warp
he held. It unsprung when
he let go. "Son, how high
will it heap?" He raked and I
crawled combing with fingers.
He made a cigarette and lit
the pile. When my mother
came running into our light
"It's alright," he said, "no use
trying to keep her anyhow."

A CURE IN CLOSE TIMES

My dad could sleep all night without smoking
except when my ear waxed hard and hurt.
Then I came, dreadfully awake in sleepers, to their bed
with a sore balloon for an ear. He rose
and made a cigarette, while I lay
down my head, aching side up. Mouth to my ear, he
dragged quick fire and said smoke in the crevices
with an aromatic and domestic warmth
in and again. I listened for the pop and wet wax
dissolving the dam. All that he whispered was
dearer than eardrops and closer than the money.

THE OUTHOUSE WAGON

Nothing had ever rolled down
between the outhouse backs.
Who would think *alley*, where
never a wheel but only Indians
ambushing Tom Mix bent down
the warm and bitter weeds, one eye
always out for praying mantises?
Never, until one early dark
washing my feet in a pan
on our back porch, I saw
how just that wagon came
making a way, first
on the telling wind, then
pressing a path that
put things in a row
and quartered my wilderness.
The horses pulled them on,
stopping behind each out-
house, the hampered lanterns
swinging dun light on shovels,
on what the wind meant, on
hands with nowhere to wipe,
the wind saying why.
The yarrows and queen-anne's lace
rose and erased the way
bruised through. But the Indians
knew, and never came back.

MORE REJOICING IN HEAVEN

Hell, Hubert Hunsecker, all Hellfire
couldn't have made me take you to the Tent
Meeting on the Fair Grounds. Gracious God
could have kept you flaming lost as Dives,
kept an abyss between you and us blessed
after your race was run if I could leap
over the ditch between our houses, Hubert,
leap over to your porch and sit while you
hauled out your leather harness for saddle soap,
to hear of heats in the Grand Circuit, and your own
standardbred you ran against Lou Dillon
and came close enough to scare all early odds
and nearly won. I liked you lost—me saved
and old enough at eight to love the Lord.

Anyway, we went, for Christ's sake and yours,
Mom and your wife serious as Sunday,
you in a Sears suit that disowned you, Dad
with his concession of a clean white shirt.
There was still dusk enough to see the stables
tall as the Gospel Tent sharing the Grounds
too close and the air where horse piss on straw
tainted the resin hope of new-thrown sawdust.
Your wife's nose narrowed, while my Mom and Dad
talked about something else, but even I
knew those lanterns and the high "Hot Damn!"
shot through the door meant poker going on.
I gave you a child's look seen and not heard
to say I wasn't fixing your salvation,
suspicious that a Hubert new in Christ
might lose all track of traps and saddle soap.
Surely you knew who prayed over tonight.
Your wife, Veena, who made you sell your standardbred horse to buy the house, Veena who sang
duets in the Loyal Philathea
Ladies Bible Circle with my mother,

and had to be married for eternity,
so saving you from the track was not enough.

It was either Sodom or Gomorrah—
one of those two fast and racy towns—
that Preacher Bassett called our county seat,
our hearts as well. He made us look and see
God shifting his brimstone from hand to hand
and hanging fire to see who would be spared.
The whole air got heavy and holding off
until everything was asking for it.
And there was the thunder then and the rainfall
and the horses saying Ha Ha among
the trumpets and the evangelist cries
"Your hands, God love you, put them up and say
yes, Larned Bassett, pray for me,
where you sit just put them up and down!"
And from the stable stompings with a neigh
break in to pick them up and put them down
against "Just As I AM Without One Plea"
and just now, clean as a starting gun
again "Hot Damn" carried across, witnessing
some stable faithful filled an inside straight
and made a joyful noise before the Lord.
You only raised your hand to wipe some sweat,
I knew, others saw Satan winded, and one
of Bassett's blessed with a zeal for souls
broke out ahead and gained along the rail
two lengths in front of others after you.
You made your move past Veena to the aisle
before those gleaners came into the stretch.
Free of the Tent, you reached the stable, where
that fellowship who'd scratched you off as lost
moved over on the bale and dealt you in.

THE ESCAPE ARTIST

"There, till you decide to be
a better citizen," she said,
"of our first grade," and jailed
him in the foot-well of her desk.
Some shoes he saw, sometimes
even socks, if the shoes came
before her desk requesting
the hall-pass to the bathroom.
No more to see, only this
baffle of three walls he hunched
inside, then one wall built of
her half-crossed legs fretted
with hosiery harnessing.
His cell smelled of old varnish,
her own must and earnest shoes.
This was nowhere to confine
his escapades she happened on.
This was no place to let be.
So he peeled a blue crayon,
molding it under his thumb
into a sled, then, eyes closed,
coasted under the panel
and kept going
to where he really was.

DIMENSIONS

God, said Spinoza, cannot care,
beyond Himself, if we are there.
He has Himself to think about,
Who, all in ALL, leaves no one out.
Whole and eternal, shall God yearn
to love Spinoza in return,
this coughing Dutch Cartesian Jew?
Utterly other. Still, these two,
Baruch and God, with a lens to grind
all evening long, seemed of one mind
while blessed geometric proof
traced the ineffably aloof.
He smiled to watch his compass span
the hopeless arc from God to Man.
"High," sighed Baruch, "but not above
the reach of intellectual Love."

Love, let from X to Y a line
conjoin your finitude with mine.
Conceive two planes inclined to seize
all tangent possibilities—
lips, fingers, even finding sweet
the intersection of our feet.
You are the given I may own.
Like Adam's wife, you can be known
and seen (without a lens). Your eyes
leave only when to my surmise.
If I have limits, so have you
(which we find pleasant proving true).
Coterminous, we draw the cry
of usual joy from X to Y.

Baruch means blessed, did you know?
For us as him, Love, be it so.

THE GOODNIGHT

Because of all that goes
without saying in the good-
night look that goes with the good-
night kiss, I often say
some commonplace to bear
the singular meaning of
our looking, still feeling
we should not separate
into our sleep without
saying how it goes.

SLEEPING DOG

Careless of pedigree, he warms the stones,
waiving with welcome noble ironies
of human circumstance, and yawning sees
when we with holocaust have bared our bones,
fetched early dark, played dead, and barked advance,
angels will pipe and little dogs will dance.

FROM AN OLD ANTHOLOGY

I scan this day our dully bred
(as I still quipping call each class),
their parcelled pages duly read.

The poem, by semestral use,
withdraws, while multifoliate
the marginalia flower profuse.

As I unravel the intent
God is not here to say, "God knows
how wide you are from all this meant."

Where once illumination lit
the letters, now mere palimpsest
whispers through rubrics grayly fit.

What once made fools of death and time
all in a likeness, nets of notes
trammel in parsing paradigm.

I've read this page for twenty years
that taught me once like light, and still
through a gloss darkly peers.

ICE FISHERMAN

He watched too many trout arc out
of his hole and lie frozen crescents
on his numbing feet. He stayed
too long, hooked by the numbers
maybe, or his careless bottle.
What little his crimp hands still
could tell him talked him off the ice.
When he happened to my fire
crisping sausage in the shore woods,
he curled like his catch around
the flames and lay till the ache
of thawing rolled him moaning
and mouthing his white fingers.

THE MUSHROOM HUNTER

"Steinpilz" old Klaus had called these,
back when Kurt ran learning
mushrooms after him. Now
a hatful of perfect ones
sauteed on the stove.
Kurt's wife and daughter kept
out on the open porch
till all were eaten.
The smell, they said.
If they had smiles and
a taste for mushrooms,
there would have been
prayer and a bottle of
Rüdesheimer with these beauties.
Now as pungently alone
as where he found them,
he only ate because
he had pulled them up and so
some good should come.

HER NOTE ON THE KITCHEN TABLE

You may find this note when you find
yourself back home whenever
having your bedtime beer despite
what time and how many already
wherever. I think I want you
to find this note. If you were
here you would hear it, if I
find where to call, I'll call
despite whoever answers. Where,
where are you now? By now
even the joints are closed. Still
this is no more crisis than tomorrow
when I'll set eggs hard over
and coffee in your white giant mug
despite whoever answered
when the joints were closed.

PROPERLY MOUNTED

Theodore Roosevelt kept his eye
on Central Park. His Indian guide
strode beside that rough rider
who stayed solidly saddled
while below boy patrons
packed the unseasonal snow and
aimed at his horse's balls.
When they hit, mothers looked
away at watches till the doors
opened at Natural History.

NOT PASSING

Compelled to come a penitential hour
early to school, and study to atone
his solid sins against geometry,
he began coming before light—seven, six—
hours no one owned, before the janitors
woke to alarms, much less unlocked the school.
Up through the open furnace room he touched
his way to those intensely empty halls.
Set in an angle of the corridor,
he nursed his mark, wishing the letter killed
a figure so incongruous to the clear
circle of God's and Euclid's unities.

While he relented there his very making,
the fountains of the deep were broken up
as every toilet bowl down all the halls
flushed like the Great Rain, and welled to Ararat.

DANCER WELL WITH CHILD

A woman with her fruit about to fall
looms low a-cumber, lady, but you seem
a horn of plenty, generous and tall.

To dance and bear—the apple tree does all
when winds reach high, and you who lofty teem,
a woman with her fruit about to fall.

Melons and plums, birth is shaped like a ball,
no splendid cone, like yours swallows would deem
a horn of plenty, generous and tall.

Another autumn for you. Like a shawl,
leaves, ready child, and pears around you stream,
a woman with her fruit about to fall.

Seeing your full gown swaying, I recall
ships under sail, grain-laden to the beam,
a horn of plenty, generous and tall.

Since once I watched you moving through the hall,
your form long ripening is all my theme—
a woman with her fruit about to fall,
a horn of plenty, generous and tall.

ONE WAY TO TELL

When she smells intimate,
my hand the coddler
warming her, brandy,
I know why noses both
smell and go crevicing,
why eyes feel their way,
the lashes cats' whiskers
measuring passage,
why lips are blindmen
knowing a sculpture,
why cheeks plane over
plain and meadow
blest with bees
when she smells intimate.

ALMOST PANTA RHEA

Heraclitus with his toe
felt the many rivers flow.
His perception was the same
with his finger in the flame.
Heraclitian flood or fire
cannot quench or burn Desire,
which drew that philosoph, I think,
to the candle and the brink.

COMPENSATION

She kept the Stradivarius, out of pride,
when her kept violinist in a run
of other music left her for a bride
younger than she, bone beautiful, and poor.

Mercifully this patroness can't hear
his consolation sounding on the bridge
of that bowed body's cordage, or the sheer
responses to his exquisite fingering.

ADMIRE THE FOX

Admire the fox who does not vault
after the muscatels on slender
tendrils, and never finding fault.
Abstainer, but no sour pretender.

Willing to lie with leaping eyes,
live with ears peaked for stems to sever,
he sucks alternatives, and wise
old bestiaries call him clever.

A man is what he lives within
and lives without. The prize of choosing
is definition. His waivers win
a silhouette edged out of losing.

Foregoing then the spoil of vines,
a vulpine Milton, he knows "Reason
also is choice," and so defines
himself the fox of figs in season.

FREE OF CHOICE

John saw himself growing old but green,
too poignant still to pardon self-denial.
He wrote excuses, pressed them with a blotter.
At the wharf's end, tied to his sundial
he leaped indulgently, and dropping gray and keen
with no end of time, he took his fill of water.

SYMPOSIUM (a drinking together)

"We're celebrating God is dead,"
he said, and filled the glasses.
I nodded. "Better dead than wed,"
I said, and cut three classes.

"We two who are about too dry
some salutary bottles
require," he said, with proofs that I
mistook for Aristotle's.

"If Life is Chaos, what is Art?"
he called across a border
of bottles. Neat I placed apart
our empties, and cried, "Order!"

"The field," he said, "is Man in Time!"
pontificating crosser.
I raised glass numbers to the prime
degree, and unread Chaucer.

Recall grew short, and we had long
forgotten what Godot meant.
Creation sang its bawdy song
that existential moment.

"No she sits here whom I'd refuse.
Warts, moles hold no abhorrence!"
he said, sprinkling our brows with brews
priestlike, invoking Lawrence.

What more than Milton can at last
guttered my gemlike burning.
Chin over textbook, I slept fast
upon that seat of learning.

WORKSHOPS

The workshops of ceramicist and bard
in corrugated tin divide the yard.
The nearness of these temporary hovels
engenders novel pots and potty novels.

****

He comes, the keening question still unspent,
an academic garret resident.
Amid symposia and art polemics
his novel's born. The question's academic.

TO JOHN TAGLIABUE

a
Word
is
precious
but
one
per
line
is
too
damn
precious.

BAPTIST EUCHARIST

His gift comes to our pews
just in remembrance said
with Welch's Grape Juice,
but the host is Wonder Bread.

BANALITY OF EVIL

He did not sell out neatly with some flair.
The thorny scruples hedging you are his.
Fat, wistful face—those lenient lines declare
the prick of conscience he endures, and is.

A TIRED ANNUNCIATION

The pill did not maternity ward off.
The patter of little foetuses beguiled
again. Once more she's, in the family way,
withstanding life with children and with child.

THE GREAT CHAIN

Professor Claudius, just promoted, hears
some coldness in the tones of former peers.
What have you, Claudius, for this chill to thank?
Says Claudius, "O my offense is rank."

DRESSING UP

A choice boy was really
invited to a real grown-up
party. He came in his genuine
Real Adult Costume
and he couldn't leave.

There was Pin the Tail and
so much Simon Says and
musical one chair less each
time and Prisoner's Base.

And so
And then

Because no one could guess
who he really was,
he won the prize and so forgot
himself until he undid
his genuine Real Adult Costume
and he really was.

HIS WONDERS TO PERFORM

That God remarks the sparrow's fall
consoles the sparrow none at all.
The stone that fells him from the fence
does not strike him as Providence.
Better no call to feel with awe
mysterious ways in fang and claw,
but perch, the one bird in the park
whom Heaven, thank you, does not mark.
Such high design it augurs, though,
to doubtless alleycats below.

A BEAST OF MIGHT AND WILL

"La bête noire du moyen age,"
the Frenchmen call that subtle beast
of discontent we can't dislodge
once possibility's decreased.

By choice the beast and I have met.
For *moyen age* I need not wait.
I choose, then in green years regret
the losses I anticipate.

The girl whose nights I will not share,
the friend whose whiskey I'll decline,
they lean prefigured on some stair
I will not climb for what is mine.

For, what is mine I must defend
against the choice I do not make,
take my child's hand, and not pretend
there's room for hands I will not take.

Perhaps the black beast does not prey
on those who both claim and refuse
all possibles, and wanton say
they really do not choose to choose.

I doubt it. Most meanders rove
where, couchant upon galling herbs,
the beast in its subjunctive grove
waits battening on modal verbs.

BY DENT OF JOY

Kliney kept the car for kicking,
to say in an express way
what dragged too late for poems.
Outside the Tempo Room he hoisted
four frugging friends to the roof
of his beat car. They danced
by sounds from the cellar.
The patrolman watched and flipped
files in his head for some ordinance,
while Kliney hummed and fit
more pennies in the meter.

LOVE'S CHAMELION

Love's Chamelion spent his prism
freely once, giving to every ground
the color of its need, taking it on
not to get lost himself, but body up
vacant shades. It was his gift to be,
out of his own possibles, the crucial color.

Buff is the best he does now, and he likes
the monotone of his terrarium.

SUDDEN FLARING

Now that his place is dark
I know he is really gone
and has been gone, I see
now, a long time, and his taking
his life, that bright implosion,
throws light on the long time
before I knew he had withdrawn
his life; we still drank together.
By now he is dense, blue and cold,
and had been long before I saw
the nova coming slow as light.

LATE NEWS

After all the weather
reports I pour the last
beer and watch
our annual flood fill
the tube's face. Enough,
always enough to see
the death through,
unlike the accidents
of love, the huddled together
improvisations of bread
given, good water and
a look. Cameras follow
help's armbands and clipboards;
they make the anomaly
normal, but the blessed
catching hold of hands
wherever is obscene
to celebrate. I turn off
the sight and stroke
the stray cat whose
shots I paid for.

WEARING WELL

What precious little does against despair.
Sun takes the ground and flourishes on stone,
I brace my heart upon the morning air.

The coffee tells, the sycamore is there,
and real things hold their places on their own.
What precious little does against despair.

The keen of questions and their edge's wear
have rasped away the night over a hone.
I brace my heart upon the morning air,

breathing it in, while it cajoles my hair
admonishing me, for I should have known
what precious little does against despair.

Night's slow erosion and the day's repair
should be familiar now. Starting alone,
I brace my heart upon the morning air.

Sufficient unto the day, to hold and bear,
life steadies in essential root and bone.
What precious little does against despair.
I brace my heart upon the morning air.

KORDAS GOING DEEP

No weedless lures or silver
lifelike dodgers for Kordas
fishing on his pond.
Simple and real worms,
lead weight and a line
to the bottom, no bobber.
"If the fish is there, he sees.
If the fish bites, I know."

Whatever takes hold
largely and plainly
he buckets in a closet
and enters his studio,
sounding his broad canvas
tight and uncertainly
bright as white-caps.
There, there again the hum
and drag of his old one.
What is ever enough?
He takes his brush
as before and wonders
what lines will hold
if he should surface.

CATECHISM

"WHAT IS THE SPIRIT OF THE BAYONET?"
We knew he knew. No sergeant is that dumb.
The question had to be a ritual.
Just yesterday we told him fifty times
as by the number, in meat-locker cold,
we lunged in lines and disembowelled the air.
My gloves stolen, I couldn't feel the stock,
much less the spirit of the bayonet.

"WHAT IS THE SPIRIT OF THE BAYONET?"
As if it were a matter of dispute.
We knew he knew. Could he perhaps forget
what was entrenched in bunkers of his mind?
Next to me Klein, whose father was a moyel,
couldn't control his bladder or his blade
and dropped out of the drill with chafing legs.
Piss on the spirit of the bayonet.

"WHAT IS THE SPIRIT OF THE BAYONET?"
We had to answer and he had to know.
Over the mike he led our litany,
constraining us to yell to save our lives.
So, having upheld painfully the same
position in this pointed dialogue,
numb to the wrist, I made my bloodless thrust
and shouted with my company, "TO KILL!"

FOR HARTMUT, FORMERLY OF HITLER YOUTH

After all broke apart
you trusted only by twos—
you and me, you and your
wife, particular ones
with sweat and their own
mouths. Between more
than four eyes grow
abstractions like NATO,
Nazis and the Great Society.
Full of second chances,
I had not beat your drum
nor sung "Horst Wessel" under flags
till rubble crowded. I was
shouting down dry wells to tell
you plans of good men
in real power. Reading the papers
now, I like to remember
our pact in Tübingen:
next time around with war
when they jail the one
the other will pass through
chocolate and cigarettes.

THE BURNING GLASS

My knock rattles rudely one more time
his office door. I hear inside where he writes
the rush of looms, the clutch of paradigms
converging, and the play of lights.

His eyes retrain on notes of their own will,
the voice comes obliquely as from a core
of Chinese boxes, though he musters still
some idioms fit for the opened door.

I feel like static interrupting news.
What do I have to tell him? Said and done,
he nods both to me and certain cues.
As I am leaving he's already gone.

CAMPO DE' FIORI
(where Bruno was burned)

"You are, passing this sentence, more afraid
perhaps, than I receiving it," betrayed,
insufferant Bruno vaunts. While dry twigs break,
into infinity they drive his stake.

Perhaps one judge, chilled with immensity,
as smoke searches up uncertainly
above the faggots' crystal crackle, hears
pole-warping and the smithering of spheres.

FINDING THE LINE

They bill you as a raree show on wire,
a high-pitched oddity in spangle tights.
What is to wonder here, except admire?
How sheer and simple can an act be made?
You walk your way with nowhere all around,
glad of so little margin. Then you stand
like Luther happy you can do no other,
or gay Newman crying, "I have a work to do
in England," from sickbed in Sicily.
A time for trumpets. How your toes rejoice
taking their order, grasping where to go
and going. These tables, bikes, umbrellas
you vaunt aloft with such high certainty
settle all doubts of how the line will bear
when things as they stand and might are poles apart.
    The wonder is I walk indifferent well.

TONGUES OF MEN AND ANGELS

Feinschmecker sliced
a gouda cheese
and spread a napkin on his knees.
He poured some porter, lightly iced,
and took his ease.

Feinschmecker placed
a midling sized
wedge on his tongue. As he incised,
beatitude was, in good taste,
palatalized.

He broke his bun.
Expectantly,
before he let the porter run,
through the glass darkly he
beheld the sun.

Feinschmecker knows:
keenly to raise
bun, cheese and porter all our days
to tongues that treat them like a rose
is also praise.